),

,

WIND

Also by Larissa Szporluk

Dark Sky Question
Isolato

The Wind, Master Cherry, the Wind

Larissa Szporluk

ALICE JAMES BOOKS
Farmington, Maine

© 2003 by Larissa Szporluk
All rights reserved
Printed in the United States

10 9 8 7 6 5 4 3 2 1

Alice James Books are published by Alice James Poetry Cooperative, Inc., an affiliate of the University of Maine at Farmington.

Alice James Books
238 Main Street
Farmington, ME 04938

www.alicejamesbooks.org

Library of Congress Cataloging-in-Publication Data

The wind, Master Cherry, the wind / Larissa Szporluk.
p. cm.
ISBN 1-882295-39-0
I. Title.
PS3569.Z66I57 2003
811'.54--dc21

2003006233

Alice James Books gratefully acknowledges support from the University of Maine at Farmington and the National Endowment for the Arts.

Cover Art: "Sleeping Giant" by Ben Wilson. Hadley Woods, Barnet, North London. Courtesy of the artist and Raw Vision Magazine.

ACKNOWLEDGMENTS

Campbell Corner Poetry Prize 2001 (finalist): "Sz," "Cat's Paw," "Contrastes," "Prodromes," "Purga," "Samiel," "Schneefresser," "Waltzing Jinn," "Tramontana"
Canary River Review: "Matsukaze"
Conduit: "Lower Egypt"
Current Magazine Poetry Award 2000: "The Adonis Fish"
Daedalus: "Death of Magellan"
Hayden's Ferry Review: "Aeronauts"
Indiana Review: "Jack-in-the-Box"
Kalliope (Sue Saniel Elkind Poetry Prize 2000): "Falter"
Landfall: "Jesus, Master of the Sea," "Fragile Little Serpent Stars," "Sub Dio," "Cauda Humana"
Luna: "Double-Crossed," "Ambulance"
Margie: The American Journal of Poetry: "Initiates' Broth," "Jubilee," "Mangiafuoco"
Meridian: "Nativity," "The Hanging"
Perihelion: "Fruit of Discord," "Memory Palace," "Guillotine"
Ploughshares: "Circling Disease," "Hippocampus"
Post Road: "Barcarole," "Sensilla"
River City: "Yellow, Singing at Night"
Smartish Pace: "Fulfilled by Parting"
Spout Magazine: "Alone in the World," "Inside the Dog-Fish," "Star of the Dance"
Washington Square: "Lerna Marsh," "Sphinx"

Special thanks to Aimee Beal, Anna Becker, Alisha Benson, Seth Berg, Paul Bissa, Abigail Cloud, Carlo Celli, Gerald Costanzo, Cort Day, Lynn Emanuel, Gayle Geider, Heidi Johannesen-Poon, Amanda Latrentra, Dana Mackowiak, Mary McGowan, Heather McHugh, Caroline Morrell, April Ossmann, Christy Palangattil, Gabriel Scala, Macklin Smith, Katharine Studer, Mary Ann Szporluk, Gianni Turchetta and the editors of the above journals, all for their enormous help and patience.

for Marco and Sofia

CONTENTS

I. FRUIT OF DISCORD

II. MINDLESS GALLOP

III. PINEAL BODY

IV. MEMORY PALACE

I. FRUIT OF DISCORD

"Those parts thus excited swell with the seed, and there is a desire to emit it towards that whither the dire craving tends; and the body seeks that which has wounded the mind with love."

–Lucretius, *De Rerum Natura*

Lerna Marsh

In the beginning there was water
and the water fussed. All reputations
have been lost. Where they lie,
there aren't kingdoms that classify
or judge. They burn in their own
scrutiny, tunics, nuptials, wings,
fluorescent children in the clutches
of the mother they've just killed—
and then the mixture hardens,
the shining tar, grains of lard,
and foul-smelling virgins, serpents,
wild boar, cleave into each other
in memoria—a hydra, in whose spit
this honey-lust for timelessness began.

Jesus, Master of the Sea

Come, swim, under.
The summer flounder compound's
in a thunder, clouds of castoff
tissue, vicious sea-cat
mother—I'm here to bless
the carnage. I'm here to answer
questions. Take my hand.
Limbs submerged
turn profoundly moving.
Bodies fugue
like lost balloons,
their indecisive down-time.
Among the bottom scour,
flora flicker off and on,
fish resemble fowl.
What's your question, Violetta?
Walking on the water?
Yes, it's fun, like perfect skin
that hides infernal candy—
who hasn't tried a pomegranate
and not belied their tongue?
But when it's done,
the breach lives on—a simple
step on solid ground
and I'm laid out, a grand capon,
trussed in my own tether.

Death of Magellan

We're struck by the sun
when it's gone;

the sure foot pauses.
Heaven was lost

when up and down
lost meaning.

Valor was lost
when all that mattered

was seeking elixir
within. The nearest star

is who we were
four years ago,

who we're not,
in terms of light,

eight years later.
The galleons, the flota,

his arm inside the armor
severed like a log—

not a day goes by
that we don't find

an unfound body
to bemoan.

Jack-in-the-Box

A mole in the gut
of an unkempt plot,
my worth isn't known.
It's not even dawn.
I hunch in my trunk.
Arthritic roosters
screech in the treetops,
driven by their fixed
prediction: *Rain*
is on the way, rain
is inevitable, rain is
infallible when falling,
ruffling the watchword
in my wired brain.
I'm told it's okay.
I'm told just to wait.
It's like laying an egg.
The sky will unflap
and the world will retch
its vertical hero—Jack,
unsung to death.

Falter

She was there in the arbor,
capillary-blue,

a butterfly, a pair of hands,
twain with wire,

nothing else for miles,
save those vines,

not even scavengers,
not one *noir*.

There was never any struggle;
her stay just broke,

and something like confectioner's
sugar sailed down,

like promises a siren makes,
her salary of bones,

bread-knives in slow motion
divvying a loaf,

or maybe shards of Easter light,
no one's fault,

or the garbled circulation
of a private thought,

the point already manifold,
a tortured note.

Circling Disease

The sum of things is the least of things.
The dwarf loved the sovereign's
daughter repeatedly:

at first, every morning, then he added on
noon, then the army honed in
like a giant umbrella.

She was carried away like a dark subject
until all that she felt and could not say
hung like a nightworld spider.

Omni et nullo. Eggs in a multiplet
structure, increasingly plump;
mother at the apogee, legs glued shut.

Fruit of Discord

Mine is a dry tree.
The sons of aliens want me.
They have a need. We all
have a need. To construct
a man made of grass
is the grass widow's need,
but she lies in the heat
of the wet tilled field,
unfulfilled, rewriting her
need. If heaven were bigger,
if hell less a machine—
are they beaming at me?
Are they singing? Someone
needs honey, someone else
cream or foam, another
needs Helen, a raw eleven,
bare-chested, hurling
stones. What is your need?
Not me? Not my worm?
Not to love what is worn?
Not to lick my sick peels
but to fuck her hard breath
in the gym? Whose side
are you on? If you want
something quick, but need it
to last, a manifest tryst,
no strings attached, pick me.
My hole is black.

Yellow, Singing at Night

the bird, wound-up,
looks almost like a lemon being shot,

the piston in its body
pumping back and forth into a blur,

like a tide that won't retire,
but hovers in remembrance of its high,

or a legendary bottle,
wrenched with genius, in the sand

where mussels secrete
amethyst tones, and the very thin rain

is a wall falling loose
at the crypt, and the song in the throat,

not rendered to stir,
stirs somehow, like a trick-maneuver

of fate, reminding him,
the boy whose palm it rivets in,

that words are not involved in this,
nor life, nor aim.

Barcarole

Hear the warning in the sleeping ice.
Too warm, too soon.

Hear the thundering
leaden heaven, the same dream,

same unalleviated anguish
echo through the grotto

like a skulk of thieves—
breaking can be golden.

Boats are knocking on the cracking water,
swans are thin with longing.

Hear them being eaten from within,
same fever, larvae, gnawing,

same honeymooning couple
supping in the muck, until what's left

of her is left of him, unconscious
fish, moving well together

now that it's not sex. A crocodile watches
from the transitory shore,

letting out a hail
of precious stones. *It's just a moment.*

Then it will be over—
the ire, and the flood of thanks.

Guillotine

Many friendships have been lost here.
It is all sky, all white, ongoing.
Faith won't save us. The date-palm
in the all-consuming sun runs its little
errand in a skirt of shade. Who said
anything about salvation? The sand diviner
lisping in the burning wind, white eyes,
white skin, converts white grains
into explicit figments: the gag at the back
of the throat, begging the throat
not to scream, the head yanked up
by the hair, upheld for the world
to see—is it possible intelligence
still dwells there? That the grosser lips
still flutter out the rhetoric of health?
That the earth hangs on nothing?
That between us, there never was a thread?

II. MINDLESS GALLOP

"In our blind seeking, we have purpose, and we suffer passion, but we never reach perception. And it is perception above all which will free us from tragedy."

—Susan Griffin, *Pornography and Silence*

P r o l o g u e

In China, Sz,
the first faint breeze
of autumn.

Cat's Paw, fainter,
lending almost nothing.

Opposed, in twos,
on afternoons,
Contrastes brush
each other.

Prodromes streak
through ancient Greece
in dog day heat.

Enter Purga,
strong northeaster,
to buffet Russia,

grim as Samiel's
hot dry slam
on Constantinople.

Schneefresser circles,
eating the snow,
sudden as an eagle
lifting a girl.

Waltzing Jinn's
grip is fiercer: a punitive
love; a drowning swimmer.

Mistral's head, a stinging bell,
stuns the south of France,

but even more alarming
is the one that drives your life,
Tramontana,
plumb out of sight,

past Matsukaze's
singing pines, whose restless
songs sway suicides.

S z

Why do you come to my house?
The two-toned trees?
Apple musk? Nostalgia?

Do you come to see the notch
that used to be the creek,
its high-speed body

curbed by scree,
not unlike our own
naïve hurry, daggered branches

shadowing our movements
like a clan of spies—
you take yourself apart,

shaken by the leaves'
omniscient cant,
Whore, whore, and like the waists

the sun pulls out of all the planets,
you whirl in the copper—
augur, aren't you?

Cat's Paw

Yonder lies a camp for the disturbed. Kids are roasting
hotdogs, singing songs. Some are clapping openly,
others in a frigid way inside. Get closer to the fire.
Whisper like an elf. One of them will give you
his whole dinner-on-a-stick. He'll watch it disappear,
the air begin to finger and divide. Then he'll dive in
after it, as if you were alive.

Contrastes

Yahweh in the thunder,
Jupiter, “the shining one,”

easting, westing,
Xerxes, near Salamis,

all those Persian bodies
silenced by the triremes,

pods of red sea lions
tossing on the beaches,

colder, softer, sunset
widows in a snowfall,

frankincense, forgiveness,
lust, a masturbator’s

picturebook, pekoe, hashish,
strokes of noon,

superboob, rhino horn,
foam, eroding knee.

Prodromes

It's not so sweet
to lose one's head,
Furia, lose one's
charge across the
dunes—the knees give
in, buckling down
of bone and skin,
Furia. Are we beast
or are we ghost,
and does this dash
toward our home
parallel Orion's own,
the reins I hold
like veins that know
how hot the neck
of this black night
must have sweat
to edge out dawn—
which we can't beat
unless we're fed
dreams or fits or even
threats in sanguine
spurts that we might
be the fastest freaks
to never leave this urn.

Purga

Depth is ahead,
not below.

Not deep like the sea,
but deep like the tips

of birches,
deep in their restlessness,

pinned by the dirt
and ice, silent as people,

deep in their silver,
shaking a little, not

touching. Deep as a figure
forced to wander,

extending the blizzard
wherever he goes—

practically winged now,
tines for feet,

eyes that weep
enamel.

Samiel

Is it possible to be different?
Exotic comes from afar.
With a bag on my head,
I fly to your plot.

In the sequel, where I fall,
I fall the way the brine
trickles down the winding snake
who rises up to man

from the bottom of the playa
to hear the echo of its name called
and hears, instead,
a hair poke through eternity,

a double sound, like tearing onion—
revelation by the bowman
that his game is dull. All the same,
a wonder girl, a birdbrain.

Schneefresser

A boy glitters,
becoming snow.

She finds him
on the mountaintop

and stays all spring
until his body melts

inside her arms.
Strawberries push up

around her feet,
daughters, small and soft,

plump with seeds.
She puts them in her mouth,

one by one. The sky,
high and still,

makes an old face.
Forgive me.

Waltzing Jinn

So goes the world.
A pigeon comes down
with fluff in her trap,
smelling of wife and ram,
and so go the herbs
that war through the garden,
enula, biondella,
gathered by Helen
the day she was stolen,
a bittersweet blond
trampled by soldiers,
the flayed-open nostrils
of lust without basis—
that's what this dance is,
the sperm of abandon,
a whale turning fragile,
a sinuous whisper
that grows, not in volume,
but toll, like the gold
on a wandering hand,
or a system of dust
that hurts less in fact
than it does to imagine.

Mistral

Where are the men now?
Circe's threshold island
of dizzying drinks,

veiled conversation.
Sleep, sleep.
Life is plain mean.

Here lie the chaste,
the sterile, the never-were
heroes, inverted

natures, dreaming of boars
stuffing their orchids
into the ample

trench of a sow, a corkscrew
tip to make her howl,
dew-claws loose

in the salty bottom…
Then a rogue of a wave,
like an awol bowel.

Tramontana

Wind is a lesson,
bringing the tongues
of chewing sheep
the blue of heaven,
eliminating illness
by changing its name
(circling, mosaic, psychic),
convincing the hermit too
by way of reason
to empty his chest,
throw out the gnomes
who bless his house
whenever they visit,
throw out the egg
whose virile yolk
smoothes his failing body
like a savage pelt;
throw it all out,
the disquieting beauty
of bizarre things,
and follow the voice
of perpetual wash
expected of him.

Matsukaze

All that is built falls at night.
The call goes out, everlasting.

Large father, how could you?
When it breaks, it's no longer

a bridge, but pillars and rivets
and glue. I thought you were

a miracle. I panic like a fish,
push the needle in—the way

to grow vague, to confound
from afar, is to rain, lose face

without having a face to begin,
like the way to the top is to be

on top to begin, time the fix,
time and again—did the man

in the moon step down to save
his drowning twin? The hang

gave way as the planks went
soft. It was such a mild winter.

III. PINEAL BODY

"Too long hast thou been untouched. Now a hand shakes thee, a hand both solicitous and playful."

—Rainer Maria Rilke, *Dolls*

Nativity

The wind, Master Cherry, the wind.
The workshop is empty.

The voice, it doesn't exist.
By heaven, don't hurt me!

The wind, Master Cherry, the wind.
Restrain this bit—*please,*

don't—reverse the grain;
give it a taste for flint,

something to live for, *don't!*
if living is what it is. Shave the outer

surface of its urge to wince;
down your wine; tuck yourself in

to the Tuscan silence,
like a tick in the musk of a beast

(or the puppet it used to be,
selfish, dreamy, festive,

up to the ears in the usual jelly),
and rest assured no one was born

this evening—no star, no king, no limb
of wood. It was only the wind,

what you think you heard—
the cry of a seasoned liar.

Initiates' Broth

A nose without end.
Dark, weak eyes
graced by the lack
of reflection.
Tongue flicking out,
mouth in a snarl.
Geppetto losing
patience. A little bit
of sun through a dirty
window; this alone,
like a drummer's lapse
into a crazy song,
keeps him going.
Brow. Neck. Hands—
snatch his yellow
jasey. *Scamp of a son!*
Respect your father!
A miserable course
to follow, as never
before in his life,
like somebody forced
to dance, a horse
to tap out math,
a monkey dressed
for war, a witness
to a stoning.

Cricket Magnificat

What could have been
a musical pet,

Learn to read
or learn a trade,

is nailed on the head
to the wall like a saint.

A shutter flaps open,
the room shrieks *Cri, cri,*

and all things killed
abnormally soon

swarm down to sing
curses, like nurses

who jab the veins
of those not afraid

not to listen,
then surge, like bats,

throughout his brain,
a killer's cave

of sleeplessness,
bewilderment, starvation.

Mangiafuoco

Now picture this—me, your wife,
a snail. Picture my insular freedom.
It snows and no one sees me
at home in my own white shoulder.

Pulcinella, Arlecchino,
beating each other with sticks;
your overly merry music
ripping through space like ice—

The Grand Puppet Theatre!
Already far from spite,
the caravan, our wooden children
strapped inside, I kissed them all

goodbye, your ruby lantern eyes
blackening behind me. Divorce.
Beard from head to floor,
whip made of fox and snake...

What would I be
if I hadn't been pitted against you?
My soul would have no furniture
to burn on a night like this.

The Hanging

Sunset is long here
falling, slipping between
the Great Oak leaves,
striking the puppet
like embers of metal,
impossibly many, impossibly
hungry, staining him
red and gold, no matter
how dull his skull is,
hissing against
his paper clothes, as if
of opinion too
that the coins in his mouth
should spit right out
into their murderous paws—
but then it is dark
at last, and the thieves
who had lain under his feet
slouch away, tired of waiting,
of watching him die
like the tongue of a bell,
mumbling, *Father, if only*,
softer, and softer,
until they could hear,
had they stayed in range,
a third, more durable
thief's acclaim.

Jubilee

Moses floated
down the winding river
in an ark of woven
reeds. He was found
by Pharaoh's daughter,
against her knee. The close
of an average morning.
An extraordinary moon-rise,
wielding a duo
of horns. Pinocchio,

in pendulum, is cut
from the hangman's
cord. Dropped
in a soft-blue carriage
attached to hundreds of mice,
he is driven like Cinderella
in a feverish parade,
her sequin gown
trailing off, like God from all
but one small leaf.

Ambulance

Four black rabbits
enter the room,
conveying a casket.

Imagine a van
turning its gas
in on the seated children,

or Zeus wiggling out
of a hurt-bird costume.
Pinocchio straightens

his back in bed.
Why did my mother
let you all in?

Why did Nemesis
welcome the eaglet
into her *grembo*?

Because he wasn't a swan,
and these are just rabbits,
not uniformed men.

What do you want from me?
—We came to take you.
A mantle of snow

covers the Jordan,
Elijah the Prophet
dividing the waters...

Pinocchio, drink it!
It's your interior country,
your faith they are after.

(Think of the staggering
egg she is big with,
the sights and the sounds

of the daughter of night
almost riding herself,
but in vain.)

Money doesn't grow like corn.
There's no such thing
as a field of miracles.

And there's no such thing
as a boy made of wood
who can talk and smoke and run,
and there are no thieves but the ones
we let—life is a comedy.

Gold is from the conscience.
If a fox and a cat
have managed to rob it,
it was already out the door,
like corporeal parts
a fly will stake
long before they're cold,
laying its eggs inside them
to expand upon the feast,
the way a butcher ties a roast
to teach the juice a lesson…

So go, little puppet, go
tell the gorilla judge
how you were a victim of fraud.
Give the names, surnames, scoop

on the long-gone thugs,
then drop your jaw to the floor
when looking-glass justice
gives *you* the cuffs.

Alone in the World

This is our slab of marble.
We died here
of sorrow, praying
that you would be good,
only good, lowing
all night like unfed
cattle drifting
through steppes
and straits. And now
we are dead, your cricket,
your Fairy, our skin
gone to tear-stain,
devotion in ruins...
A huge Roman snail
will answer a door
in the terrible future
and hand you a bowl
of unreal fruit.
And then you will know
forgiveness is over,
just as the cypress
high above Garda
laughs at its silver face,
never thinks twice
about messenger doves
or whether or not
it was fathered.

Donkey Fever

Friendship torn apart by whips,
never mind a false one—*Lucignolo!*
Suddenly the rustling of ghosts,
cotton-candy wrappings, like unreceived
bouquets, floating across the dust,
and suddenly the world on its foretold
fire: *l'Omino,* smiling,
physiognomy of milk and honey,
having lured all the boys away
from Latin, curfew, chores,
having teamed his midnight buggy
with salt-and-pepper burros
whose wet beast eyes still look at him
with disbelieving fervor—
l'Omino, the little man of butter,
stirring nausea and promises
like *riso* in *minestra.*

Star of the Dance

The circus is as bright as day.
The famous donkey Pinocchio
leaps through flaming hoops
in four white boots,
his hide as lustrous as a mirror.
His hair has been curled,
adorned with roses—in truth,
he's an ass to be in love with.

The ring-leader raises an arm,
fires a pistol. The star
feigns being shot, slumps
to the earth as if truly morbid,
this to a flood of applause.
The Fairy, high in the stands,
is wearing his portrait
brooched to her throat.

Trying to reach her, he trips,
is lamed, sold to a drunk
who needs skin for a drum.
Blind-folded, hurled, tied
to a stone, a sun withdrawing
shine—how droll to see him
drown, the cord yanked up
like a riled viper.

Inside the Dog-Fish

Wide as the church, the sea, the cavern,
hard as a rock, a tree, a geyser, tight
as the spot of birth, hot as the furnace,
serpent, witch, plain as the ego, primitive,
tomb, loose as a swallow's whirling torso,
fiery vertebra—*madre terribile*, mother
of agony, atony, urge, providing a passage,
a sabbath, excuse, symbol of charm
gone darkly sour, emotional windbag
pricked by the light of the *luna cornuta*,
spitting up trinkets and bottles of rum,
and pages of books, and chunks of men.

Fulfilled by Parting

The harlot in the desert
plaits herself a collar

to keep her spirit low.
In a time of slower swings,

more expansive budding,
the sudden manic flower

hits the ground.
Things can't help

being what they are:
the tallest house of cards,

the most seductive armor—
Puppet, are you out there?

Is your incubation monstrous?
Will you lose your holy flit

in all that flesh?
The snail begins to run

like a fireball in August,
not a thought about her ragged

shell. The navigator, home,
completely settles down,

slips into the mouth she left
of semi-conscious yarn.

IV. MEMORY PALACE

"It was mine art that made gape the pine and let thee out."

—William Shakespeare, *The Tempest*

Aeronauts

What do the gossamer spiders gain,
paying out millions of threads,
heads to the winds, covering meadows?
There is this or that yearning.
Here comes a girl with a gill for a lung
crossing the morning, moving like truth
into story, clear as vermouth, *enough,*
gelatinous tongue, *enough, enough*,
riding a goat or the tip of a wave;
what does she gain by spilling her guts,
a long gluey streak, like a sail
in her wake, that could have been used
to pick up speed, or tease a bull,
or rise above the walls of her asylum.

Fragile Little Serpent Stars

It's a dance,
the whole life,
the life coming down,

years that were stupid,
and then some, a man,
wasted, wasted

lacrime, tears, the crime,
a hair-salted child,
a narrow canal,

daughter named wisdom,
son with a mark,
third in Elysium,

losing my facts,
dumber than a box
of rocks, diamonds,

rubies, onyx,
things that grow bright
when we lose them,

vermiculite, toxins,
illuminated vomit
of a mountain, my lover

on fire without me—
flat on my back
on the combed earth,

a sow sucked of milk—
in his smoldering mouth,
the new bolt.

Hippocampus

A bell is gonged,
the body of a girl
curled up inside it,

a town grown wild,
dogs sniffing skyward—
gong, gong.

They listen all night
for the girl to fall,
her stomach to growl,

the foundered skirt
to hop and swell,
a gallows flower,

or is it a foot
in a mindless gallop,
snorts of delight

as the gods take up
the virgin-offer,
or is it a weird

and beautiful gargle,
the lovemaking sound
of a deep-sea diver?

The Adonis Fish

There is peace between us
when we're sleeping.
Even the wavelets
beating my face
are soothing my brain.
Odd how the giant bird
becomes dear friend
in Hades, as do
arrow, discus, boar,
dying so young, dying beautiful,
as does father become lover
in his drink, or lover,
father, in his likeness,
as do I, divided between
mothers, natural and captor,
sea and land,
slip from womb to wooden
chest without a cry—
woe to Adonis, me, me,
sleeping in the spirit
with my mother named for
myrrh, or with my lovers
in her likeness on a bed
of butter lettuce,
thumping out a symphony
of lips and tails that dulls me,
me, Adonis, without enemies
of men, only women
enemies who love me.

Sub Dio

A weeping giant, a troll, an awful drill,
they take her by the hand
to a clearing in the forest
where the strawberries are wan with frost
and the fringe of resin pines
huddles, plainspoken…

Your goose is lined with gold.
If I were you, I'd cut her open.
Listen to the farmer do it.
His conscience flaps and squirms
in a whirligig of voices
as he vivisects the egging place,
the gall of which, ye rubbernecks, is ordinary…

Wee little woman,
your wee little bone
is tethered to a clause
that condemns to death removal
by the living of the aforesaid
from the jaws of what is ghost
and lawful owner, neither great unwashed
nor thoroughbred exempt…

Let it be said, sub dio.
Why are the heavens irregular?
Hell pulls down. For pleasure,
a breast will be lifted and passed like a plum
in a pantomime of feasting,

but half of its cup is stone; the dynamo
electric can't remember who
converted whom:
cacophony, the golden bird, the cuboid,
every holy beauty in the world...

Cauda Humana

The rat is a sign
of descent. The crow
is farewell, liberation.
These are just monkeys
who lost their tails
in a brief evolution
that sweetened and joined
them, like snow white
gloves or ebony plums,
or childhood homes
that weren't romantic
but shaped them.
It shaped them. Masons
in chains, linked
like rings, the mystical
systems of objects
on water, the marvelous
laughter that carries
a sinner on continuous
journeys of empty and full—
Time to move on, the men
tell the women. *We live*
to relive, the women
reply, dipping their insides,
swishing from heights,
strung-out in clusters,
reared to fight.

Sensilla

Moon-fish sing with their teeth,
grinding their incisors.

The runaway young,
in a place that hurts,

ask themselves out loud,
Is that father at the bottom,

calling, singing, grinding?
Will he find us?

All the little hairs,
membranes, labyrinths,

pores, all the little
fluid-filled tubes and spirals

in the world cannot save them
from the shark.

If only they would petrify,
erasing every pressure wave,

like chicks that stiffen
in the chicken-hawking shade,

instead of this paroxysm
some call dance—

danza macabre,
impulse that the body makes

to call upon the afterlife
to wrestle it away.

Sphinx

This luxurious chest. This way-side
manner. This raised eyebrow
at this next passer.
What has varying feet and a voice?

This pause. This breeze.
This faint retsina. Voice,
voice of what? What voice over time
doesn't change?

What time? What change? What work
in obscurity, this mind taking out
its rage on this face,
as if this were an answer.

Lower Egypt

Roused by the honey
of dawn, the drone,
Not many things
come back to life,

fixed like a piece of ice
to the moistest calyx,
but love does,
war does, hunger does,

remembers the queen,
and queens do,
kings do,
lust inching up,

an idea to plunder;
but once in full mount
on the flower,
once the hot breath

of the cobral Nile
fatigued by the plunge
into tang too familiar,
makes the pink granite

islands look real...
he relaxes his feeler,
exits her head.
Death was better.

Memory Palace

A cloud takes a lifetime
to smother the sun. It's finally

a crime, but it's also a glory,
the lining sizzling gold,

the afternoon's image
occulted. Truth is I don't

have an art. One pulls the other
one down. I know

there's a blue-purple hill.
I know all the girls

disappear. I don't
break a sweat. I sit

the whole year with a bird
on my lap. The firmament

wobbles. Their deep
purple feet. Asleep, it comes

back, fast, but late—
there were poisonous leaves

and salt on the path
like an alphabet.

NOTES

p. 19: *Prologue* was inspired by the glossary of winds in *Heaven's Breath*, by Lyall Watson.

p. 39: *Mangiafuoco* means *fire-eater*; it is the name of the puppeteer in *The Adventures of Pinocchio*.

p. 42: *Ambulance*: *grembo* is *lap* in Italian. The title echoes that of a short Polish film about the Holocaust, referred to briefly in stanza two.

p. 47: *Donkey Fever*: Lucignolo is the name of Pinocchio's roguish friend (Lampwick in Disney's English version); *l'Omino*, the carriage-driver, means *little man*; *riso* is *rice*; *minestra* is a vegetable soup.

p. 56: *Fragile Little Serpent Stars: lacrime* is Italian for *tears*.

Recent Titles from Alice James Books

North True South Bright, Dan Beachy-Quick
Granted, Mary Szybist
My Mojave, Donald Revell
Sails the Wind Left Behind, Alessandra Lynch
Sea Gate, Jocelyn Emerson
An Ordinary Day, Xue Di
The Captain Lands in Paradise, Sarah Manguso
Ladder Music, Ellen Doré Watson
Self and Simulacra, Liz Waldner
Live Feed, Tom Thompson
The Chime, Cort Day
Utopic, Claudia Keelan
Pity the Bathtub Its Forced Embrace of the Human Form, Matthea Harvey
Isthmus, Alice Jones
The Arrival of the Future, B.H. Fairchild
The Kingdom of the Subjunctive, Suzanne Wise
Camera Lyrica, Amy Newman
How I Got Lost So Close to Home, Amy Dryansky
Zero Gravity, Eric Gamalinda
Fire & Flower, Laura Kasischke
The Groundnote, Janet Kaplan
An Ark of Sorts, Celia Gilbert
The Way Out, Lisa Sewell
The Art of the Lathe, B.H. Fairchild
Generation, Sharon Kraus
Journey Fruit, Kinereth Gensler
We Live in Bodies, Ellen Doré Watson
Middle Kingdom, Adrienne Su
Heavy Grace, Robert Cording
Proofreading the Histories, Nora Mitchell
We Have Gone to the Beach, Cynthia Huntington
The Wanderer King, Theodore Deppe
Girl Hurt, E.J. Miller Laino
The Moon Reflected Fire, Doug Anderson
Vox Angelica, Timothy Liu
Call and Response, Forrest Hamer

Alice James Books has been publishing exclusively poetry since 1973. One of the few presses in the country that is run collectively, the cooperative selects manuscripts for publication through both regional and national annual competitions. New regional authors become active members of the cooperative, participating in the editorial decisions of the press. The press, which historically placed an emphasis on publishing women poets, was named for Alice James, sister of William and Henry, whose fine journal and gift for writing went unrecognized within her lifetime.

Typeset and Designed by Dede Cummings
Printed by Thomson-Shore